#GOALS

LIFE BEHIND THE INSTAGRAM FILTER

#GOALS

From Instagram to Twitter, we all want to be a social media star these days. But behind your phone screen, are those perfectly filtered lives all they're really cracked up to be? For millennials everywhere, here comes a book that says what we're all really thinking. Whether it's stuffing your face with pizza while scrolling through Gigi Hadid's feed or experiencing life at the speed of fifteen WTFs per hour, this is the real life struggle of getting *that* double tap and achieving #goals.

#GROWNUPGOALS

In my defence, I was left unsupervized.

Being an adult is like trying
to fold a fitted sheet.

Don't cry over spilt milk.
It could have been gin.

The path to inner peace
begins with four words:
Not my fucking problem.

Life is not a fairy tale.
If you lose your shoe at
midnight, you're drunk.

Taking a nap sounds so childish.
I like to call them
horizontal life pauses.

Let us have a moment
of silence for all the things
we added to our cart but
never bought.

I think my guardian
angel drinks.

Maybe swearing will help?

People who wonder whether
the glass is half full or half
empty are missing the point.
The glass is REFILLABLE.

I would like to confirm that
I do not care.

Some days I amaze myself.
Other days I put my
keys in the fridge.

When you're trying to
take a nap and you hear
people outside, making noise,
living life…

I am currently experiencing
life at the speed of 15 WTFs
per hour.

'Be strong'
I whisper to my wifi signal.

Just waiting patiently for
that dislike button.

Sometimes I have to unfollow
people in real life.

I'm nicer when I like my outfit.

#RELATIONSHIPGOALS

Nap dates should be a thing.

Morning sex when
you're hungover.
High five.

Never date a boy who wears skinnier jeans than you.

That accidental double tap...

FYI
I don't look very good
in the morning.

I'm going to take you not
caring about farting in front
of me as a compliment.

When you don't even
have to fake it.

As emotionally stable
as an ikea table.

Sometimes we're so damn cute I think we could be an Instagram couple.

Nobody puts bae
in the corner.

I actually shaved my legs.
I must really like you.

When you make great food together and give yourselves Michelin stars.

I would love you more
if you were pizza.

Oh, there are plenty of
fish in the sea?
Yeah, well none of them
want to date you either.

I can hear you rolling
your eyes at me.

Let's cuddle so I can
steal your body heat.

We're only dating because
I want your followers.

Let's get day drunk together.

#BEAUTYGOALS

When you haven't worn makeup for a week and then you put on mascara.

This bitch is back.

I did *not* wake up like this.

I got 99 hairgrips but
I can't find one.

Too glam to give a damn.

Just wing it.
Life, eyeliner,
everything.

Maybe she's born
with it. Maybe it's an
Instagram filter.

I came.
I saw.
I contoured.

The only drama I enjoy
is in my lashes.

Eyebrows.
The only thing I can get into
shape without exercising.

Life isn't perfect, but
your hair can be.

Nails before males.

I could stop buying makeup,
but I'm not a quitter.

Staring at girls who
have no pores like damn,
I'll have what she's having.

Dry shampoo is the
new shower, right?

Liquid eyeliner can
sense your fear.

It's not you,
it's your eyebrows.

My lip balm dependency
is getting out of hand.

Boy: Let's get naked.
Me: Which palette?

#FOODGOALS

I want to be like a caterpillar.
Eat a lot. Sleep for a while.
Wake up beautiful.

Breakfast for dinner.

I spend a lot of time holding
the fridge door open
looking for answers.

I just don't want to look
back and think
'I could've eaten that'.

Eating cereal straight
from the box.

The only man I'll ever run after is the one who drives the ice cream van.

Don't tell me that hunger
isn't an emotion because I feel
that shit in my soul.

FIT(ish): Semi fit; Kinda fit; someone who likes the idea of being fit but also reeeally likes food.

Eat the spaghetti to
forgetti your regretti.

If I made poached eggs
and didn't Instagram them,
did I really even make
poached eggs?

I'm just a girl, standing
in front of a salad,
asking it to be a donut.

I'm in a serious relationship
with carbs.

My favourite kind of coffee
is the kind where no one talks
to me while I'm drinking it.

I like hashtags because
they look like waffles.

I followed my heart and it led me to the fridge.

If your coffee order is longer than four words then you are part of the problem.

An apple a day keeps anyone away if you throw it hard enough.

Don't go bacon my heart.

#WORKGOALS

So it turns out being an adult is mostly just googling how to do stuff.

Nothing ruins Friday more
than realising it's
only Tuesday.

Group projects make
me realise why Batman
worked alone.

Word of the day:
Exhaustipated (adj); too
tired to give a shit.

The hardest part of my
job is being nice to
stupid people.

Maybe I'll just be
instafamous instead?

The first five days after
the weekend are always
the hardest.

Almost adulting.

Due to my current workload
the light at the end of the
tunnel will be turned off
until further notice.

I've used up all my sick days
so I'm calling in dead.

Friyay!

Mornings are stupid.

Another fine day ruined
by responsibility.

I just don't understand
how everyone is always
on holiday.

I'm not feeling very worky.

I bet I could be a really
good blogger.

Me: I don't wanna go to work.
Bills: Bitch better have
my money.

Sometimes the best part of my job is that the chair swivels.

#SQUADGOALS

We've been friends
so long I can't remember
which one of us is
the bad influence.

Wine o'clock.

A real best friend makes
your family question
your sexuality.

If girls treated each other the way they do in club toilets the world would be a much happier place.

We'll be the old ladies
causing trouble in the
nursing home.

I guess you're allowed to
have other friends...
You just have to love
me the most.

Good friends
don't let you do
stupid things...alone.

I don't know what's tighter.
Our jeans or our friendship.

You're my lobster.

I feel bad for the people who don't get to hear how hilarious we are.

We go together like drunk
and disorderly.

If you got stung
by a jellyfish I would
totally pee on you.

If you don't drink,
how will your friends know
you love them at 2am?

I swear to always pretend
to be your lesbian lover when
someone weird hits on you.

It's remarkable
how long we've
tolerated each other.

Talking at the
speed of light.

A true friend only
posts photos that you
both look good in.

We're going to
have so much fun in
hell together.

#BODYGOALS

Scrolling through
Gigi Hadid's insta feed
while eating pizza.

I was hot until my Photoshop
free trial expired.

The best way to lose weight is to only eat inspirational quotes.

Why be moody when you can shake your booty?

My favourite exercise is
something between
a lunge and a crunch.
Its called lunch.

That awkward moment
when you're wearing
Nikes and you actually
can't do it.

Does running out
of eyeliner count
as cardio?

Good times
and tan lines.

Just saw three people
jogging outside.
It inspired me to get up
and close the blinds.

Dear extra fat in my body,
you have two options:
make your way to my
boobs or GTFO.

I ate salad AND went
for a run today.
I better be skinny
tomorrow.

Be a bad ass with
a good ass.

Ok it's been 4 years now.
I'm starting to think I'm not
just bloated.

Savasana please.

My body, my rules.

I hope your day is as
nice as my butt.

A wise woman once said 'fuck this shit'. And she lived happily ever after.

#THEEND

Publishing Director Sarah Lavelle
Editorial Assistant Harriet Webster
Designer Maeve Bargman
Words Harriet Webster
Production Director Vincent Smith
Production Controller Jessica Otway

Published in 2018 by Quadrille,
an imprint of Hardie Grant Publishing

Quadrille
52-54 Southwark Street
London SE1 1UN
quadrille.com

Text © Quadrille Publishing 2018
Design © Quadrille Publishing 2018

ISBN 978 1 78713 228 3

Printed in China